getting
to
good

getting
to
good

A GUIDED JOURNAL

Bring Happiness and Positivity into Your Day

Elena Welsh, PhD

Illustrations by Kath Nash

ALTHEA
PRESS

For my sons, who remind me
to see the magic
in the world every day.

Interior and Cover Designer: Suzanne LaGasa
Photo Art Director: Sue Bischofberger
Editor: Melissa Valentine

Production Editor: Andrew Yackira
Illustrator: Kath Nash

ISBN: Print 978-1-64152-366-0

R1

This book belongs to:

INTRODUCTION

Most of us, at some point or another, enter phases of life when we want to feel better. My guess is that if you're reading this book, there's a part of you that needs to heal.

Perhaps you've been feeling down, or overwhelmed, or a bit lost. Maybe you have that nagging sense that something's missing from your life. Or maybe you've been dealing with symptoms of depression or anxiety. Whatever it is, know that it's perfectly normal to experience periods of sadness, melancholy, and even hopelessness. Reaching for this book is a sign that you're ready to invite more positive emotions into your life.

Research shows that positive emotions allow us to think more creatively and freely, which helps us develop more novel solutions to life's challenges. So in the midst of pain and suffering, if you can cultivate some sense of joy, gratitude, or laughter, you're more likely to thrive in the face of hardship. Mind you, the goal is not to avoid feeling sadness or other difficult emotions such as fear, jealousy, or anger. Rather, you want to make room for positive emotions to arise and coexist with the pain. Feelings are meant to be felt. If you avoid feeling difficult emotions or shove them away, they will find a way to be heard—often in more extreme and damaging forms. At the same time, if you dwell or fixate on negative emotional states to the extent that there's little space to feel anything else, you'll only fuel their fire, sparking them to grow bigger and more consuming.

The pathway to healing is cultivating an attitude of positivity and gratitude. This doesn't always come easily, but the good news is there are many simple steps you can take to reach this path, many of which are supported by science and contained in the following pages. Some of these steps include focusing your attention toward the things that are going well in your life, learning how to live more fully in the present moment, catching yourself when you exaggerate how bad things are, and noticing and shifting unhelpful thought patterns. Even small steps like these can lead you to somewhere better.

I know this firsthand from my work as a licensed clinical psychologist. In my practice, I work with all types of clients who are experiencing depression, anxiety, or trauma, or simply seeking a richer life. The exercises and strategies contained in this book draw from effective therapeutic modalities such as Cognitive Behavioral Therapy, Positive Psychology, Motivational Interviewing, and Mindfulness. These are the same techniques that have worked for my therapy clients and that I use myself when I'm feeling down or struggling to feel satisfied and fulfilled.

In my work as a therapist, I've been continually struck by how our thoughts, habits, and attitudes have the power to shape our life experience. I've worked with people who seem to "have it all" in terms of jobs, friends, and resources, but who are plagued by worries, low self-esteem, and feelings of worthlessness. I've also worked with clients who on the outside appear to have very little, such as those who are incarcerated or homeless, but who thrive by developing healthy and happy thought patterns and a deep sense of appreciation for life. Whatever your circumstances, your mind has the power to help you cultivate the life you want to live.

As you dive into these pages, please keep in mind that this book is not a cure for depression. It is not meant to replace treatments for mental health difficulties. Instead, it serves as an important supplemental tool for your journey toward feeling better. Expressing and exploring emotions through writing has been shown to lead to emotional relief and increased feelings of happiness. The following prompts and exercises will help you shift your mind-set in order to feel more peace, contentment, and joy, regardless of what's happening around you.

I recommend turning to this book daily and working your way through it, start to finish.

If you feel more inclined to skip around, that works, too. The key is consistency—the more regularly you return to this book and the strategies contained within, the more benefits you will experience.

Give yourself permission to start feeling better today. You can build a life you love—starting now.

"There are always flowers for those who want to see them."

—Henri Matisse

Write down **10** things you are **grateful** for right now:

1. _____

2. _____

3. _____

4. _____

5. _____

6. _____

7. _____

8. _____

9. _____

10. _____

These are a few of my **favorite** things:

People:
_____
_____
_____
_____

Places:
_____
_____
_____
_____

Activities:
_____
_____
_____
_____

Foods:
_____
_____
_____
_____

Sounds:
_____
_____
_____
_____

Write down at least one **favorite** thing from your day for **a week** straight:

DAY	FAVORITE THING
Monday	
Tuesday	
Wednesday	
Thursday	
Friday	
Saturday	
Sunday	

What **I love** about **my life**:

_____

_____

_____

_____

_____

_____

_____

_____

_____

_____

_____

_____

_____

_____

_____

_____

_____

_____

_____

_____

_____

What **I love** about **myself**:

_____

_____

_____

_____

_____

_____

_____

_____

_____

_____

_____

_____

_____

_____

_____

_____

_____

_____

_____

Ask **three people** you're close with to tell you something they
like about you. Record their responses below:

NAME:

NAME:

NAME:

Complete the following prompt with a **positive affirmation**.

I AM:

_____

Now copy this affirmation on a small piece of paper or Post-it Note and hang it in a spot where you'll see it daily, like on your bathroom mirror or fridge. For one week, every time you see the note, repeat it to yourself (ideally aloud). Next week, pick a new affirmation and repeat this exercise.

What does **gratitude** mean to you? Does it come easily? Or is it **something you have to work at**?

_____

_____

_____

_____

_____

_____

_____

_____

_____

_____

_____

_____

_____

_____

_____

_____

_____

_____

Write about something **you** are **looking forward** to.

List **five people** you are **grateful** for and why:

Tell those people you are grateful for them and **why**.
How did it **feel** to tell them? Reflect below.

Write about something that made you **laugh** this week.

"There are only two ways to live your life. One is as though nothing is a miracle. The other is as though everything is a miracle."

—Albert Einstein

Write about a few **small miracles** you have **witnessed** recently.

_____

_____

_____

_____

_____

_____

_____

_____

_____

_____

_____

_____

_____

_____

_____

_____

_____

_____

_____

_____

_____

_____

Spend some time outside in a place you find beautiful, like the beach, the mountains, or your favorite spot in your own backyard. Watch the sunrise or sunset. Take a moment to really contemplate how magical the world can be.

List **five things** that regularly make you **smile**.

Where do **you feel** most **peaceful** and **safe**?

Close your eyes and **picture that place** in as much detail
as possible. What are the sights, sounds, colors, and smells?

_____

_____

_____

_____

_____

_____

_____

_____

_____

_____

_____

_____

_____

_____

_____

_____

Look around you right now. What are you grateful for in your current surroundings?

_____

_____

_____

_____

_____

_____

_____

_____

_____

_____

_____

_____

_____

_____

_____

_____

_____

_____

_____

Write about a recent **adventure** that left you feeling **inspired** or **energized**.

_____

_____

_____

_____

_____

_____

_____

_____

_____

_____

_____

_____

_____

_____

_____

_____

_____

Start each **morning** this week by writing down
three things you're **grateful** for.

DAY	GRATEFUL FOR
Monday	
Tuesday	
Wednesday	
Thursday	
Friday	
Saturday	
Sunday	

"The world only
exists in your eyes.
You can make it as
big or as small
as you want."

—*F. Scott Fitzgerald*

Imagine that your **life** is exactly how **you want it to be**.
Write in detail about what it looks and feels like.

_____

_____

_____

_____

_____

_____

_____

_____

_____

_____

_____

_____

_____

_____

_____

_____

_____

_____

_____

_____

_____

_____

What is **one small step** you could take this week to get you even an inch **closer** to your ideal life?

_____

_____

_____

_____

_____

_____

_____

_____

_____

_____

_____

_____

_____

_____

_____

_____

_____

_____

Think about the **happiest** time in your life from the last five to ten years. **Write about it in the present tense, as if it were happening now.** Describe it in as much detail as possible, including the emotions you're feeling, who you're with, and where you are.

_____

_____

_____

_____

_____

_____

_____

_____

_____

_____

_____

_____

_____

_____

_____

_____

_____

_____

Look back on the last two pages and circle every **positive** thing or emotion. Write them down below. Next to each positive word, **write one action you can take today** to experience that same emotion again.

_____

_____

_____

_____

_____

_____

_____

_____

_____

_____

_____

_____

_____

_____

_____

_____

List **ten things** that you have always **wanted to try**, but haven't yet.

1. _____

2. _____

3. _____

4. _____

5. _____

6. _____

7. _____

8. _____

9. _____

10. _____

List what **fuels** you in the following areas:

Love:

_____

_____

_____

Happiness:

_____

_____

_____

Courage:

_____

_____

_____

Purpose:

_____

_____

_____

Fun:

_____

_____

_____

Relationships:

_____

_____

_____

_____

Start each morning this week by writing down a
positive intention for the day. For instance:
"Today, I will listen to my body," or *"Today I will put others first."*

Monday:

_____

_____

Tuesday:

_____

_____

Wednesday:

_____

_____

Thursday:

_____

_____

Friday:

_____

_____

Saturday:

_____

_____

Sunday:

_____

_____

Put on your favorite song
and dance freely.
Repeat until you are smiling.

Set an alarm for a particular time each day for a week. Every time the alarm rings, pause and think of something you're grateful for.

Take a picture
of something
beautiful today.

What aspects of your current life are focused on **fulfilling dreams** and **desires** of your past? Is it time to **let** any of these dreams or desires **go**?

_____

_____

_____

_____

_____

_____

_____

_____

_____

_____

_____

_____

_____

_____

_____

_____

_____

_____

"Start where you are. Use what you have. Do what you can."

—*Arthur Ashe*

YOU ARE HERE

Write out **three of your goals** or dreams in the **present tense**, as if you've **already achieved** them. Write in as much detail as possible in order to begin to feel what it's like to already be there.

_____

_____

_____

_____

_____

_____

_____

_____

_____

_____

_____

_____

_____

_____

_____

_____

_____

_____

Fill the toolbox below with the **resources you have** (people, things, skills) that can **help** get you **where you want to be.**

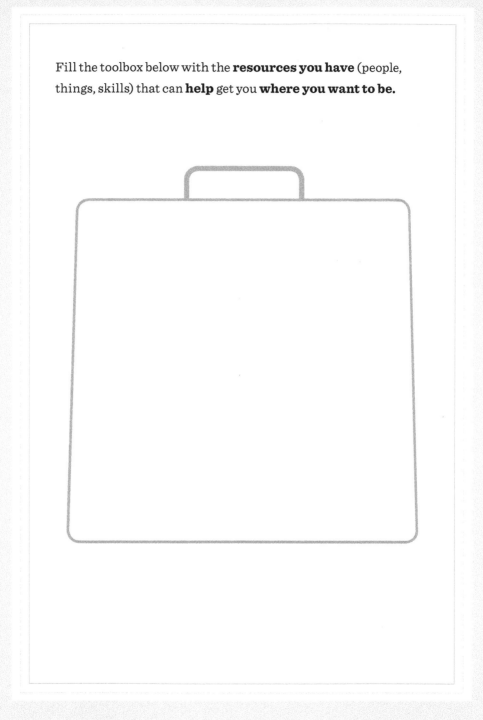

Write about how you've made a **lasting** impact on the world. If you feel stuck, think small. In what ways have you shown someone **kindness** or created something **beautiful**? Reflect on how this could have a lasting impact, no matter how small.

_____

_____

_____

_____

_____

_____

_____

_____

_____

_____

_____

_____

_____

_____

_____

_____

_____

_____

_____

_____

_____

_____

Write about something you **learned** this week.

_____

_____

_____

_____

_____

_____

_____

_____

_____

_____

_____

_____

_____

_____

_____

_____

_____

_____

_____

_____

Move Your Body!

Pick a different **physical activity** to engage in each day this week and record them below.

Monday: ☐
_____

_____

Tuesday: ☐
_____

_____

Wednesday: ☐
_____

_____

Thursday: ☐
_____

_____

Friday: ☐
_____

_____

Saturday: ☐
_____

_____

Sunday: ☐
_____

What are you **really good** at? Write freely about as
many things as you can think of.

_____

_____

_____

_____

_____

_____

_____

_____

_____

_____

_____

_____

_____

_____

_____

_____

_____

_____

Write about how you think **someone you love** would **describe you**.

_____

_____

_____

_____

_____

_____

_____

_____

_____

_____

_____

_____

_____

_____

_____

_____

_____

_____

"Wisdom means to choose now what will make sense later. I am learning every day to allow the space between where I am and where I want to be to inspire and not terrify me."

—*Tracee Ellis Ross*

Fill in each circle with your **goals** in each area of your life. Lightly color a portion of the circle to represent how much progress you have already made in this area. Let the unfilled areas of your circle **inspire** instead of frighten you.

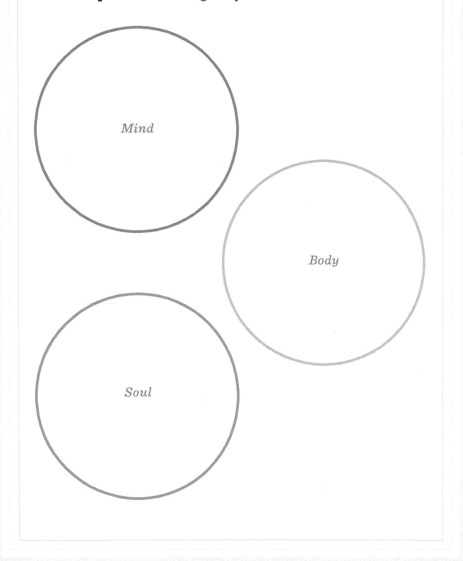

Mind

Body

Soul

Imagine yourself on one side of a bridge and **happiness** on the other side. What's the stuff in the middle that's keeping you from **crossing that bridge**? Write it in the space below the bridge.

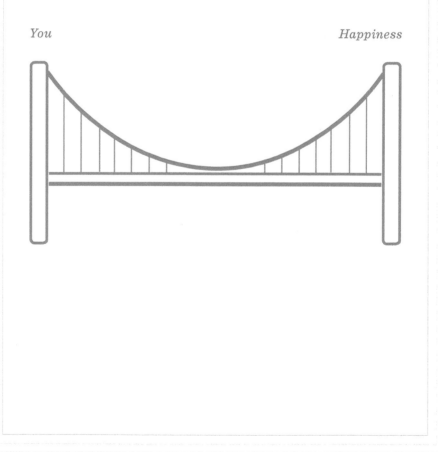

You

Happiness

Think about the **values** that are most important to you, and rank them accordingly in the chart below. There's also room to fill in a few of your own. Next, consider whether you are **living in line with these values**, and rate yourself in the "Action" column.

VALUE	IMPORTANCE*
Family	
Friends	
Work	
Learning	
Fun/Recreation	
Spirituality	
Health/Fitness/Wellness	
Community	
The Environment	
Beauty/Aesthetics	

* **How important each value is to you.** Rate on a scale of 1 to 10, with 1 meaning *"not very important"* and 10 meaning *"very important/a deeply held value."*

_____

_____

_____

_____

_____

_____

_____

_____

_____

_____

** **How much are your daily actions in line with your values?**
Rate on a scale of 1 to 10, with 1 meaning _"I wish I were doing much more in this area,"_ and 10 meaning _"I'm living in line with this value."_

Pick one of the values that you rated as highly important to you on page 56, but that is not as high on the action scale. **What can you do** this week to **start living** in line with this value?

_____

_____

_____

_____

_____

_____

_____

_____

_____

_____

_____

_____

_____

_____

_____

_____

_____

What type of **friend** are **you**?

_____

_____

_____

_____

_____

_____

_____

_____

_____

_____

_____

_____

_____

_____

_____

_____

_____

_____

_____

_____

What type of **friend** do you **want to be**?

_____

_____

_____

_____

_____

_____

_____

_____

_____

_____

_____

_____

_____

_____

_____

_____

_____

_____

_____

In what ways are you **already** the type of **friend** you want to be? In what ways can you **begin** to be the type of friend you want to be?

_____

_____

_____

_____

_____

_____

_____

_____

_____

_____

_____

_____

_____

_____

_____

_____

_____

_____

_____

_____

Complete the following writing prompt:

I am grateful for my friendship with

_____

because . . .

_____

_____

_____

_____

_____

_____

_____

_____

_____

_____

_____

_____

_____

_____

Circle the **feelings** you most often feel.

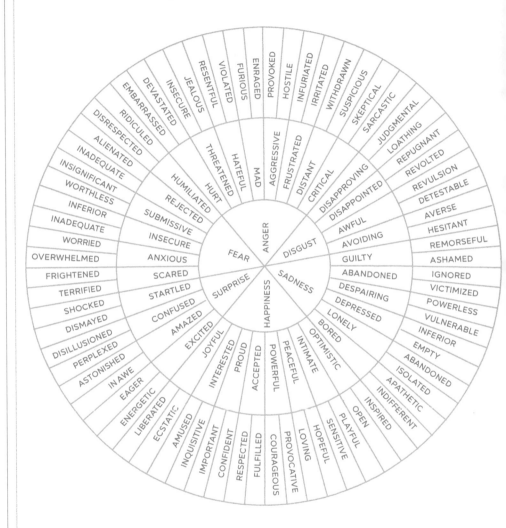

Now, cross out the feelings you want to feel less and color in the feelings you want to feel more often.

What feelings do you want to feel **more** often?

_____

_____

_____

_____

_____

_____

_____

_____

What can you do to **increase** these feelings in your life?

_____

_____

_____

_____

_____

_____

_____

_____

who I Am Versus Who I Want to Be

Rate yourself in the following areas:

Brave ⟵——————————————————⟶ *Fearful*

1   2   3   4   5   6   7   8   9   10

Kind ⟵——————————————————⟶ *Unkind*

1   2   3   4   5   6   7   8   9   10

Giving to others ⟵————⟶ *Taking care of myself*

1   2   3   4   5   6   7   8   9   10

Patient ⟵—————————————⟶ *Impatient*

1   2   3   4   5   6   7   8   9   10

Present ⟵—————————⟶ *Living in the past or future*

1   2   3   4   5   6   7   8   9   10

Open to new experiences ⟵————⟶ *Stuck in my ways*

1   2   3   4   5   6   7   8   9   10

Now, choose a different color pen and rate where you want to be in each area.

Pick one of the areas on page 66 and write about how you can work to **embody** **more of the qualities you aspire to have**.

_____

_____

_____

_____

_____

_____

_____

_____

_____

_____

_____

_____

_____

_____

_____

_____

_____

_____

List **five emotions** you would like to $feel$ today. Next, write a corresponding action you could take to increase the chances of feeling each emotion.

List **5 emotions** you are hoping to **avoid** today. Next, write a corresponding action you could take to decrease the chances of feeling each emotion.

"We are what
we repeatedly do.
Excellence, then,
is not an act,
but a habit."

—*Aristotle*

Pick **one small thing** you can **commit** to doing every day for **30 days** that you know will make you **feel better**. Examples include taking a walk, drinking eight glasses of water, or starting the day with a short gratitude list.

I commit to

_____

every day.

1	2	3	4	5	6	7
8	9	10	11	12	13	14
15	16	17	18	19	20	21
22	23	24	25	26	27	28
29	30					

Repeat this exercise next month with a new commitment.

Write freely about something that is **bothering** you.

Read through the previous page. Circle everything that is within your control and cross out anything that isn't. Write down the list of things **within your control**, and next to each item write down the next step you can take to begin to **tackle** or **change** it.

_____

_____

_____

_____

_____

_____

_____

_____

_____

_____

_____

_____

_____

_____

_____

_____

_____

_____

Things Within
My Control

Action
I Can Take

How were you **kind** to **yourself** today? Reflect on this question below.

_____

_____

_____

_____

_____

_____

_____

_____

_____

_____

_____

_____

_____

_____

_____

_____

_____

_____

_____

_____

How were you **kind** to your **body** today? Reflect on this question below.

_____

_____

_____

_____

_____

_____

_____

_____

_____

_____

_____

_____

_____

_____

_____

_____

_____

_____

Write down **10 things** that make you **happy**.

1. _____

_____

2. _____

_____

3. _____

_____

4. _____

_____

5. _____

_____

6. _____

_____

7. _____

_____

8. _____

_____

9. _____

_____

10. _____

_____

Do one of those things today.

If you were the **best possible** version of yourself, what would that look like? What would you be doing more of? What would you be doing less of?

_____

_____

_____

_____

_____

_____

_____

_____

_____

_____

_____

_____

_____

_____

_____

_____

_____

_____

_____

_____

"Promise me you will not spend so much time treading water and trying to keep your head above the waves that you forget, truly forget, how much you have always loved to swim."

—*Tyler Knott Gregson*

What makes you **feel most fully** alive?

_____

_____

_____

_____

_____

_____

_____

_____

_____

_____

_____

_____

_____

_____

_____

_____

_____

_____

_____

_____

How can you do **more** of what makes you feel alive?

_____

_____

_____

_____

_____

_____

_____

_____

_____

_____

_____

_____

_____

_____

_____

_____

_____

Is there something **important** to you or some part of you that has gotten **lost in the busyness** of your daily life? Write freely about what that is and how you might **get it back.**

_____

_____

_____

_____

_____

_____

_____

_____

_____

_____

_____

_____

_____

_____

_____

_____

_____

_____

_____

_____

_____

Are there things in your life that you often think will make you happy, but **don't really**?

_____

_____

_____

_____

_____

_____

_____

_____

_____

_____

_____

_____

_____

_____

_____

_____

_____

_____

_____

How can you begin to **let** some of these **things go**?

_____

_____

_____

_____

_____

_____

_____

_____

_____

_____

_____

_____

_____

_____

_____

_____

_____

_____

_____

_____

Below or on a separate piece of paper, **make a collage of images** that make you feel **happy** and **inspired**.

Imagine you are nearing the end of your life. What things do you wish you spent **more time** doing?

_____

_____

_____

_____

_____

_____

_____

_____

What things do you wish you had spent **less time** doing?

_____

_____

_____

_____

_____

_____

_____

_____

Are there any **changes** **you want to make** based on the reflections on page 88?

_____

_____

_____

_____

_____

_____

_____

_____

_____

_____

_____

_____

_____

_____

_____

_____

_____

_____

_____

_____

Characteristics of **Happy People**

Below are some characteristics that are common among people who are happy. **Circle any that you possess.**

Hopeful

Humorous

Optimistic

Adaptable

Kind

Energetic

Good Listener

Grateful

Positive

Cooperative

Curious

Honest

Confident

Spontaneous

Authentic

Nice

Next, pick **three** of the characteristics **you possess** and write about how you can use these characteristics to become even happier.

_____

_____

_____

_____

_____

_____

_____

Pick **one or two characteristics** you didn't circle and write about how you might **cultivate** these in your life.

_____

_____

_____

_____

_____

_____

_____

What is your favorite **inspirational** quote?

Write it here:

_____

_____

_____

_____

_____

_____

_____

_____

_____

_____

_____

_____

_____

_____

_____

_____

_____

_____

Write about a **time in your life** when you felt **inspired**.

Write about a time in your life when you felt like you were **right where you were supposed to be**.

_____

_____

_____

_____

_____

_____

_____

_____

_____

_____

_____

_____

_____

_____

_____

_____

_____

_____

_____

_____

GRATITUDE MEDITATION

Sit in a comfortable position with your
eyes closed. Take a deep breath.
Instead of trying to clear your mind,
take the next few moments to reflect
on everything you are grateful for.
If other thoughts creep in,
acknowledge them and let them go,
then shift your attention back
to your gratitude.

"There are only two days in the year that nothing can be done. One is called yesterday and the other is called tomorrow, so today is the right day to love, believe, do, and mostly live."

—*His Holiness the Dalai Lama*

Pick **one of your five senses** and use it as a tool today to bring you back to the **present moment**.

Write about **something nice** that you noticed today, something that caught your attention due to being aware of that particular sense. Do you think you would have noticed it otherwise?

_____

_____

_____

_____

_____

_____

_____

_____

_____

_____

_____

_____

_____

_____

_____

_____

_____

_____

Write your worries on a piece of paper.
Next, rip the paper up into tiny
pieces, safely burn it, or fold it so
many times you can no longer see
the writing. Visualize releasing
the worries as you go.

Write **freely** about something that is **bothering** you.

What **advice** would you give a **friend** or **loved one** going through the same thing that you wrote about on the previous page?

_____

_____

_____

_____

_____

_____

_____

_____

_____

_____

_____

_____

_____

_____

_____

_____

Place your hand on your stomach.
Take a deep breath in and exhale
fully (you should feel your hand
rise and fall with your breath).
Repeat.
Try to keep your mind
in the present moment.
When it begins to wander
(and it will!), gently return
your focus to your breath.

Write about a **time in your life** when you felt at **peace**.

_____

_____

_____

_____

_____

_____

_____

_____

_____

_____

_____

_____

_____

_____

_____

_____

_____

_____

_____

Be a tourist in your own town.
Pick an activity you would do if you
were visiting for the first time.
Is there anything well known in your
town that you haven't visited or
experienced yet? Check it out!

"Vulnerability sounds like truth and feels like courage."

—*Brené Brown*

Write about a time in your life when **you spoke your** truth, despite feeling **scared** or **vulnerable**. How did it feel?

_____

_____

_____

_____

_____

_____

_____

_____

_____

_____

_____

_____

_____

_____

_____

_____

_____

_____

_____

_____

_____

Is there currently an area in your life where you wish you could be more **authentically** you? What's holding you back?

_____

_____

_____

_____

_____

_____

_____

_____

_____

_____

_____

_____

_____

_____

_____

_____

_____

Write about a time you were **vulnerable** with someone and, as a result, you felt **closer** to them.

TAKE A SELF-CARE DAY

Spend a day pampering yourself in whatever fashion sounds best to you. Eat your favorite foods, relax, take a bath, get a massage, read a book—whatever nourishes you inside and out.

LOVING-KINDNESS MEDITATION

Begin in a comfortable seated position. Place your hand over your heart and take a deep breath in and out. Recite the following verses aloud or to yourself:

May I be free from suffering.

May I experience pure joy.

May I be at peace.

May [name someone you love] *be free from suffering.*

May [name someone you love] *experience pure joy.*

May [name someone you love] *be at peace.*

May [name a person you have had difficult interactions with] *be free from suffering.*

May [name a person you have had difficult interactions with] *experience pure joy.*

May [name a person you have had difficult interactions with] *be at peace.*

May all beings be free from suffering.

May all beings experience pure joy.

May all beings be at peace.

Write about a **time** when you felt **brave**.

Write about a **time** when you felt **loved**.

_____

_____

_____

_____

_____

_____

_____

_____

_____

_____

_____

_____

_____

_____

_____

_____

_____

_____

_____

_____

_____

"Don't compare your life
to others. There is no
comparison between the sun
and the moon. They shine
when it is their time."

—*Unknown*

What makes you **uniquely** you?

_____

_____

_____

_____

_____

_____

_____

_____

_____

_____

_____

_____

_____

_____

_____

_____

_____

_____

Is there a person or type of **person** you often compare
yourself to and feel like you fall short? What part of them do
you particularly **admire**?

Who **inspires** you and why? Write down their names and what you **appreciate** about them. They can be friends, family, or even public figures.

_____

_____

_____

_____

_____

_____

_____

_____

_____

_____

_____

_____

_____

_____

_____

_____

Of the attributes of those you admire, circle the attributes that you also possess.

How I Want to Be

_____

_____

_____

_____

_____

_____

_____

_____

_____

_____

_____

_____

_____

_____

_____

_____

_____

_____

Why I Want to Be This Way

_____

_____

_____

_____

_____

_____

_____

_____

_____

_____

_____

_____

_____

_____

_____

_____

_____

_____

What are the things you **do not want to** change about yourself?

_____

_____

_____

_____

_____

_____

_____

_____

_____

_____

_____

_____

_____

_____

_____

_____

_____

_____

MEDITATION:
WATCHING YOUR THOUGHTS GO BY

Take a deep breath in and exhale.

Imagine that your mind is the sky and

your thoughts are the clouds drifting by.

Notice each thought as it drifts by,

but don't hold on to it.

Let it drift in and out of your mind.

Complete the following writing prompt.

I am **grateful** for who I am because...

_____

_____

_____

_____

_____

_____

_____

_____

_____

_____

_____

_____

_____

_____

_____

_____

_____

_____

"Only in the
darkness can you
see the stars."

—*Martin Luther King Jr.*

Write freely about a particularly **challenging** time in your life.

_____

_____

_____

_____

_____

_____

_____

_____

_____

_____

_____

_____

_____

_____

_____

_____

_____

_____

_____

_____

Now, write about everything you learned from the difficult time you described on the previous page. In what ways are you stronger? How has your **perspective** on the situation changed?

_____

_____

_____

_____

_____

_____

_____

_____

_____

_____

_____

_____

_____

_____

_____

_____

_____

Write about a time when you faced something hard, but there was a **surprise silver lining** and you ended up with a **new beginning**.

Hard Day To-Do List:

Add more "to-dos" to this list on a day when you are feeling good. The next time you have a hard day, force yourself to go through this list, even if you don't feel like it.

☐ Get outside

☐ Move my body

☐ Call a friend

☐ Take a deep breath

☐ Gently remind myself to stay in the present moment

☐

☐

☐

Write about something that is **bothering** you.

_____

_____

_____

_____

_____

_____

_____

Do you think this problem will matter to you five years from now? If so, what are some ways you can **minimize** the impact of the problem? If not, is this something you can let go?

_____

_____

_____

_____

_____

_____

_____

_____

Go outside and
look at the moon and stars.
Make a wish upon a star.

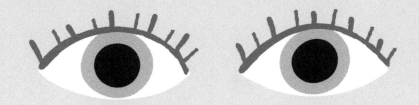

"At first glance it
may appear too
hard. Look again.
Always look again."

—*Mary Anne Radmacher*

CREATE A WORRY WINDOW

Schedule 5 to 15 minutes today to WORRY. During that period of time, worry, worry, and worry some more. Then stop. If you start to worry outside of your scheduled worry time, remind yourself that you are outside of your worry window and you must save it for later. Repeat daily, as needed.

Write about a time in your life when you struggled but
didn't give up.

_____

_____

_____

_____

_____

_____

_____

_____

_____

_____

_____

_____

_____

_____

_____

_____

_____

_____

_____

Consider a problem you have been approaching **logically** but are still struggling with. If you approach it with more of your **heart** and **soul**, can you find a **new perspective** on the problem?

_____

_____

_____

_____

_____

_____

_____

_____

_____

_____

_____

_____

_____

_____

_____

_____

_____

_____

Write about a **positive change** you know you want to make in your life.

_____

_____

_____

_____

_____

_____

_____

_____

_____

How **ready** are you to make this change?

Not at all ready ←————————————→ _Totally ready_

1   2   3   4   5   6   7   8   9   10

How **motivated** are you to make this change?

Not at all motivated ←————————→ _Totally motivated_

1   2   3   4   5   6   7   8   9   10

How **confident** are you that you can make this change?

Not at all confident ←————————→ _Totally confident_

1   2   3   4   5   6   7   8   9   10

How did you get to where you are in terms of your **readiness**, **motivation**, and **confidence** to make the **change** you wrote about on the previous page?

_____

_____

_____

_____

_____

_____

_____

_____

_____

What would make you more **ready**? More **motivated**? More **confident**?

_____

_____

_____

_____

_____

_____

_____

_____

"Be careful of your thoughts, for your thoughts become your words. Be careful of your words, for your words become your actions. Be careful of your actions, for your actions become your habits. Be careful of your habits, for your habits become your character. Be careful of your character, for your character becomes your destiny."

—*Chinese proverb*

Have you had any of these **thoughts** **about yourself** lately?

☐   I suck.

_____

☐   I'm not good enough.

_____

☐   I can't do that.

_____

☐   What's the point?

_____

☐   Nobody cares anyway.

_____

☐

_____

☐

_____

☐

_____

☐

_____

What would your **friends** or **loved ones**
tell you about the **thoughts** you checked off on the previous page?

_____

_____

_____

_____

_____

_____

_____

_____

What would **you** tell a friend who is having these **thoughts**?

_____

_____

_____

_____

_____

_____

_____

_____

Stinking Thinking

Everyone falls into distorted or extreme thinking from time to time. The problem is, these types of thoughts often lead us to feel bad. Do you recognize any of the following thought patterns? Check any that apply to you. The next time these arise, try to "catch and correct" before falling into their trap.

☐ **Black and white thinking:** Everything is either all good or all bad, with no in between.

☐ **Negative focus:** When you focus on only the negative aspects of a situation, while ignoring or minimizing the positives.

☐ **Fortune telling:** Predicting that negative things will happen in the future, without knowing for sure.

☐ **Mind reading:** When you assume someone is thinking something negative about you without having any evidence or really knowing what they are thinking.

☐ **Catastrophizing:** When you exaggerate how bad something is going to be and its potential effect on your life.

☐ **Emotional reasoning:** When you let your mood dictate your thoughts. Because you are feeling bad or sad, you assume that bad things will happen.

List some of your specific frequent **negative** thoughts below.

_____

_____

_____

_____

_____

Can you categorize any of these thoughts within the common forms of **Stinking Thinking** (page 137)?

Catch and Correct

Now, write out some counterarguments to these thoughts. They don't have to be entirely positive, but try to be grounded in reality and take a less extreme or exaggerated approach. What else is possible? What are the facts? Are there **positive** aspects of the situation?

_____

_____

_____

_____

When you catch yourself engaging in these forms of Stinking Thinking, remind yourself of these counterarguments. The more you practice, the easier it will be to "catch and correct" before negative feelings take root.

Sit in a comfortable place. As you take a deep breath in, imagine that you are breathing in positivity, love, and happiness. As you exhale, imagine that you are releasing negativity, judgment, and suffering.

Write freely about the past week. How did you **feel**?
What happened? What was **good**? What was **challenging**?

_____

_____

_____

_____

_____

_____

_____

_____

_____

_____

_____

_____

_____

_____

_____

_____

_____

_____

_____

_____

_____

Underline every **fact** you wrote on the previous page about the past week. Cross out anything that was **speculation** or based on **perception**. Write what is left here.

_____

_____

_____

_____

_____

_____

_____

_____

_____

_____

_____

_____

_____

_____

_____

_____

_____

_____

What are your **five** most frequent **thoughts**?

_____

_____

_____

_____

_____

_____

_____

_____

_____

_____

_____

_____

_____

_____

_____

Cross out any of these thoughts that are not helpful to you.
Replace them with thoughts you wish you had more often.

Write about a **difficult** situation that you encountered today.

_____

_____

_____

_____

_____

_____

_____

_____

_____

_____

_____

_____

_____

_____

_____

_____

_____

_____

_____

_____

What is the **first thought** that came to your mind about the situation you recounted on the previous page?

Is your thought extreme or exaggerated in any way? Did your mind overreact at all? Rewrite a **more balanced and positive** version of your thought below.

_____

_____

_____

_____

_____

_____

_____

_____

Stop "Should-ing" on Yourself!

List **five thoughts** you have about your life that include the word **should**.

Rewrite the statements on the previous page to **get rid of "should."** (For example, *"I should be married,"* becomes *"I would like to get married someday."*) Review the revised statements. How do they feel now?

"Not all of us can do great things, but we can do small things with great love."

—*Mother Teresa*

Smile at as
many people
as possible today.

Do something **kind** (a small or large act) for someone you love today.

Write freely about how it made you feel to complete this **act of kindness**.

_____

_____

_____

_____

_____

_____

_____

_____

_____

_____

_____

_____

_____

_____

_____

_____

Engage in a random act of
kindness today, without knowing
what the outcome will be or
who your kindness will touch.

*Some ideas include: hiding five dollars or an encouraging note
in a common place, leaving change near a vending machine or
wishing fountain, delivering flowers or handwritten cards to a
hospital, or sending a care package to a soldier. Take a moment
to imagine the joy you might have brought to the world.*

Think of five **compliments** that you can **give to others** this week.

Write about a time when someone in your life stepped up in a way that really meant something to you or **changed** your life for the better.

_____

_____

_____

_____

_____

_____

_____

_____

_____

_____

_____

_____

_____

_____

_____

_____

_____

Let that person know how much you appreciate them. Call, email, or write to them this week.

Write about **something kind** you did for
someone else in the past week.

Share your best **advice** in **one sentence**.

_____

_____

_____

_____

_____

_____

_____

_____

_____

_____

_____

_____

_____

_____

_____

_____

_____

_____

Complete the following writing prompt:

I am **grateful** for my **family** because ...

_____

_____

_____

_____

_____

_____

_____

_____

_____

_____

_____

_____

_____

_____

_____

_____

_____

Daily Kindness Log

For one week, vow to do acts of kindness each day. Start with one act of kindness on Monday and increase daily until you reach seven acts of kindness on Sunday.

DAY	ACT(S) OF KINDNESS
Monday	
Tuesday	
Wednesday	
Thursday	
Friday	
Saturday	
Sunday	

Write someone a **letter** and tell them why you're **grateful** for them.

Dear

_____

Thank you for . . .

_____

_____

_____

_____

_____

_____

_____

_____

_____

_____

_____

_____

_____

_____

_____

_____

"If you ever find yourself
in the wrong story, leave."

—*Mo Willems*

What **part(s) of your life** do you want to **rewrite**?

How can you start this **new chapter** today?

_____

_____

_____

_____

_____

_____

_____

_____

_____

_____

_____

_____

_____

_____

_____

_____

_____

_____

_____

What are you ready to **leave** behind?

_____

_____

_____

_____

_____

_____

_____

_____

_____

_____

_____

_____

_____

_____

_____

_____

_____

_____

_____

_____

Rate the following **areas of your life** in one color, with 1 being not so great and 10 being excellent. Pick another color and indicate where you **hope** to be in each area in the next few months.

Mood

1   2   3   4   5   6   7   8   9   10

Health

1   2   3   4   5   6   7   8   9   10

Social Life

1   2   3   4   5   6   7   8   9   10

Purpose

1   2   3   4   5   6   7   8   9   10

Relationships

1   2   3   4   5   6   7   8   9   10

Work

1   2   3   4   5   6   7   8   9   10

Finances

1   2   3   4   5   6   7   8   9   10

Fun

1   2   3   4   5   6   7   8   9   10

Service

1   2   3   4   5   6   7   8   9   10

Pick three areas in your life on the previous page where there is the greatest **discrepancy** between where you are and where you want to be. What can you do to **get closer** to where you want to be?

_____

_____

_____

_____

_____

_____

_____

_____

_____

_____

_____

_____

_____

_____

_____

_____

Imagine you are living in the **future** in a life that you love. Write yourself a letter from your future self. What helped get you there? What advice do you have for your present self?

Dear Self:

_____

_____

_____

_____

_____

_____

_____

_____

_____

_____

_____

_____

_____

_____

_____

What would your **childhood self** think of your life today?
In what areas are you making that child **proud**?
In what areas would that child wish more for you?

_____

_____

_____

_____

_____

_____

_____

_____

_____

_____

_____

_____

_____

_____

_____

_____

_____

_____

Characteristics of **Successful Changers**

Below are characteristics that are common among people who can successfully make important life changes. Circle any that you possess.

Committed   *Strong*

Optimistic

Resourceful

Clever

Flexible

Patient

Relaxed

Forgiving   *Hopeful*

Wise

Open

Humble

Thoughtful

Persistent

Pick three of the characteristics you circled on the previous page and write about how they can help you make an **important** **change** in your life.

CHARACTERISTIC:

CHARACTERISTIC:

CHARACTERISTIC:

Write about something from your **past** that feels like a roadblock to your happiness.

How can you **overcome** the roadblock you wrote about on the previous page?

_____

_____

_____

_____

_____

_____

_____

_____

_____

_____

_____

_____

_____

_____

_____

_____

_____

_____

_____

Write about something from your **present** that feels like a roadblock to your happiness.

_____

_____

_____

_____

_____

_____

_____

How can you **overcome** this?

_____

_____

_____

_____

_____

_____

_____

_____

_____

What are you passionate about? How do your passions inform your **daily life**?

_____

_____

_____

_____

_____

_____

_____

_____

_____

_____

_____

_____

_____

_____

_____

_____

_____

_____

"May your choices reflect your hopes, not your fears."

—*Nelson Mandela*

Write about a time when you let your **fears** dictate your choices. What can you **learn** from that experience?

How do your **hopes** and **dreams** inform your
purpose and daily choices?

_____

_____

_____

_____

_____

_____

_____

_____

_____

_____

_____

_____

_____

_____

_____

_____

_____

_____

Write about a **change** that you want to make in your life, but that you are **struggling** with.

_____

_____

_____

_____

_____

What are the pros and cons of making this change?

Pros   # Cons

_____   _____

_____   _____

_____   _____

_____   _____

_____   _____

_____   _____

_____   _____

_____   _____

_____   _____

_____   _____

Write about a **dream** you have that has not come true **yet**.

_____

_____

_____

_____

_____

_____

_____

_____

_____

_____

_____

_____

_____

_____

_____

_____

_____

_____

_____

_____

_____

Fill in the box below with some of your **greatest fears**. Next, color over the words or glue or tape beautiful images on top of them, until you can no longer see the words or they are **transformed** in some way.

Write about something that is making you **anxious**.

_____

_____

_____

_____

_____

_____

_____

_____

_____

_____

_____

_____

_____

_____

_____

_____

_____

_____

_____

_____

_____

What is the **worst** thing that could happen?

_____

_____

_____

_____

What is the **best** thing that could happen?

_____

_____

_____

_____

What about something **in between** the best and the
worst things that could happen?

_____

_____

_____

_____

My Hopes and
Dreams

Choices I Can Make to
Support Them

_____   _____

_____   _____

_____   _____

_____   _____

_____   _____

_____   _____

_____   _____

_____   _____

_____   _____

_____   _____

_____   _____

_____   _____

_____   _____

_____   _____

_____   _____

_____   _____

_____

Write about a time when you **surprised** yourself and felt unexpectedly **proud**.

"Believe you can and you're halfway there."

—*Theodore Roosevelt*

Write down three great things that you would like to happen this week. Next to each one, write something that you can do to **make it a reality**.

Write the next chapter of your life. How do you want it to unfold? What **dreams** and **wishes** can you make come true?

_____

_____

_____

_____

_____

_____

_____

_____

_____

_____

_____

_____

_____

_____

_____

_____

_____

_____

What doubts are **holding you** back?

_____

_____

_____

_____

_____

_____

_____

_____

_____

_____

_____

_____

_____

_____

_____

_____

_____

_____

_____

_____

_____

Write the doubts from the previous page on a piece of paper. Next, rip the paper up into tiny pieces, safely burn it, or fold it so many times that you can no longer see the writing. Visualize yourself releasing the doubts as you go.

Write about a time when you **transformed** your life or an aspect of yourself.

_____

_____

_____

_____

_____

_____

_____

_____

_____

_____

_____

_____

_____

_____

_____

_____

_____

_____

_____

_____

Write one of your **strengths** in each section of the circle below.

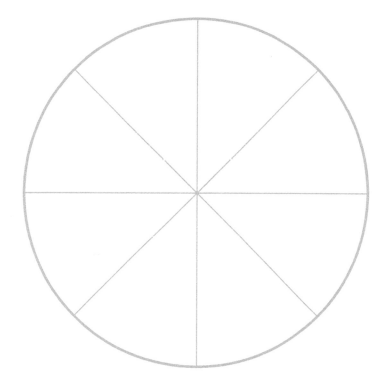

Contemplate how fully you're using each of your strengths, and color in the spaces accordingly. (So, if you are fully using a given strength, that section of the circle will be fully colored in. If you aren't regularly using a particular strength, that section will be partially shaded.)

Examine the underused (partially shaded-in) strengths on page 187. How could you **tap** into these strengths more fully?

_____

_____

_____

_____

_____

_____

_____

_____

_____

_____

_____

_____

_____

_____

_____

_____

_____

_____

_____

Write about some of the **best choices** you have made in your life so far.

_____

_____

_____

_____

_____

_____

_____

_____

_____

_____

_____

_____

_____

_____

_____

_____

_____

Remember, you always hold the power to make good choices!

MORE RESOURCES
FOR YOUR JOURNEY

Authentic Happiness: Questionnaire Center

AuthenticHappiness.sas.upenn.edu/testcenter

Provided by the University of Pennsylvania, this website offers multiple free questionnaires and surveys based on the principles of Positive Psychology. The questionnaires provide insight on a variety of topics, including signature strengths, sources of meaning, and happiness and life satisfaction.

Calm

Calm.com

This highly-rated app provides guided meditations and other strategies to calm your mind and body.

Gratitude Garden App

iTunes.Apple.com/us/app/gratitude-garden/id1101115763?mt=8

This free app provides a platform for gratitude journaling. Each time you record something positive, it rewards you with points to build a gratitude garden.

Live Happy

LiveHappy.com

This helpful website recommends articles, books, movies, blogs, and podcasts, all focused on the theme of finding authentic happiness.

ABOUT THE AUTHOR

Elena Welsh, PhD, is a licensed clinical psychologist. Dr. Welsh received her doctorate degree from the University of Maryland, Baltimore County, and completed advanced clinical training through a postdoctoral fellowship at Gateways Psychiatric Hospital in Los Angeles. Dr. Welsh works with a wide range of clients who experience depression, anxiety, or trauma, or are simply seeking a richer life. She has published articles in various medical and research journals and is the author of *Trauma Survivors' Strategies for Healing: A Workbook to Help You Grow, Rebuild, and Take Back Your Life*. Dr. Welsh also serves as an adjunct faculty member at Antioch University, Los Angeles. She lives with her husband and two young sons in Los Angeles, California.